REVERSE ENGINEER

KATE COLBY

ORNITHOPTER PRESS   PRINCETON

First Edition

Published by Ornithopter Press
www.ornithopterpress.com

ISBN 978-1-942723-12-7

Library of Congress Control Number: 2022932973

Cover painting: L.S. Lowry, *Girl Seen from the Back*, 1964
© The Estate of L.S. Lowry. All Rights Reserved, DACS / ARS 2022

Design and composition by Mark Harris

CONTENTS

Doubting I love while knowing I've wanted to.

—Rosmarie Waldrop

REVERSE ENGINEER

GEODUCK

A wrinkled sheet
of sunlit sea, fat

flat-bottom clouds
crowd the horizon.

Conditions of the world
are cumulative—all
I can say about it is.

If I could see past
curvature, I would tell

what's there
left to know.

•

Am I a common
member of my species?

House cat, crow, pigeon,
whose drab plumage

serves it as well as any
comely summons.

Only I need to
know I'm seen

a glass being
filled with rain

tracks my mirror image.

·

So far the world is
as long as I think—

stars tick
a round face

day lasts
all the way.

Clear as dark
on a black sand beach

no light's discrete
the better to see

this bright bivalve

two-sided lines
run around.

UNEXPECTED BEING

A kind of presence—

what took all of
time to arrive at

the rest will never get here.

Words are full
of dark meaning,

meaning without
proof of matter.

As a baby jams
a square in the star hole

a simile works
like this.

•

Words are like a container
ship full of empty containers—

all I can see is the shape
that takes it.

What will come after
me is what I'm after,

systemic failure of
systems meaning both

"birds-eye" and a bird's eye,
a black hole.

ACTUARIUM

Who's to say when
the world will end

by which I mean
which one? Today

the city's viscous
with distance

the river bends into it.

Twice it gives
the ocean back

(which is broken,
the cork or the neck).

There's only this
to go on.

•

In some points of light
a manufactured weakness,

perforations to plan
where you'll break.

Lean from the window
as far as you can see

an empty lot
full of weeds.

We are born double-blind
to fill the darkness in.

       •

The whole world is
unique to each of us—

the form of a field
is growing.

Words turn into
a revolving door

that admits itself
(a great occasion

is a great occasion,
and so forth).

SAINT NAMESAKE

What I can't understand
about my mind

is what it's doing here

the way waves break
on facing shores.

My body has a name
that's the shape of it,

distance is its limit—

as a train leaves the tracks behind
my wake was here to begin with.

•

How high goes the night sky,
the depth of my property line?

All I know is
what my head holds

holds me back.
(Am I repeating myself?)

In a room of one's own
viewless window:

orange mesh
construction fence.

Infinity is "to be"
without me.

ARSE POETICA

Herein the question
of what a poem is is

more important than
what it says. That said,

no poem ever fails
to extemporize

its reason for being
what is essentially itself.

●

Trees smear
train window

more immediate
forehead grease

(what I write about the everyday is
not my experience of the everyday)

a vestigial armrest ashtray.

●

A genome isn't made
of letters—this is

hard to remember.

Narrows, shallows, knee
pockets, sockets I can't see

the back of, my body is half
a map and the rest is history.

What I can't know
beyond recollection

I put into words
to see how it seems.

INTEGER*

1.

Wind can't move the light
only what's in front of it.

Stirring shadow-
shaped leaves

or dead specimens
in Plexiglas? *Dodo*

is a word, a museum
of museums.

2.

Every time I hear "Rocket Man"
I'm reminded of you

reminded of me
every time you hear "Rocket Man."

3.

*A thing complete in itself.

All that I can see from
the distance of the sun

the moon has broken
up with its light.

I was caught, kissed
in the teeth of a time-

worn cemetery—

love isn't real
only how you feel it.

AFTER LIFE

Everything I think
to say is never true

anymore—the medium
of thinking is thought.

If all possible worlds
exist and we're in

the best one, will you be
awake when I get home?

The day we put the dog down
I felt my *umwelt* like anything

admitted by emptiness
excepting itself.

DUPE

Two precepts of artificial
intelligence on television:

never show a computer
its code; and the more

a robot understands, the less
likely it is to know

it's not real.
I am nothing if not

aware the self is made
the shape that explains it—

the purpose of living
is to keep alive

what I should know
I should know.

DIRECTIONS TO FOLLOW

Home is where
you put it there—

any place
but here.

If I knew
then what
I know now

there is no center
of its breadth.

         •

The furthest place
I've never been next to

me, poor creature
cooked in its ink,

doesn't know
the dark there.

The heart is off-
center, my brain

wouldn't pick it
from a lineup.

What I think
sounds like me—

a cake knife
made of cake

knife.

●

I wish I knew what
I said in my sleep

a lost thing
I keep losing.

Ran the wrong way
through a footrace, breathing

starfield in my face.
A cumulative wound

I open to bones—how far
beneath us goes the ground.

The body left
a night-filled house

to wake the same
shape as clouds.

NIGHT VISION

Shadows are ideas
of what casts them;

the moon is there
to match, but only

on one side. Stars
pick through leaves,

a tree-shaped black
space swallows itself.

If I could disgorge
my heart like a star-

fish its stomach
I'd draw you in,

but I only have this head
and how I love you

looks more like me than I do.

PEDIMENT

Does a cave grow or get left behind?
Is the capacity of a balloon the same

when inflated? Interminable
questions pack into a chasm

I keep for you—

the hole we
hold together.

Through winter I see
each snow-articulated twig

convey it like a cup
across the floor

of the room you bring to me.

There are no doors,
only jambs standing in for.

AIR LOCK

Form is what
we share the world with—

a wave that doesn't
take the water with it.

Only you contain me,
like a sieve sorts the sea.

We hold our heads
in each other's hands

found our air Atlantis

the key to which breaks
the lock by breaking in it.

STILL BORN

Two things are always equi-
distant—the room not there

before you—

a view that describes
the eye to it.

Norman Bates's mother
(the cutout one, in the window)

is the silhouette she made you.

Time doesn't take so long
as you're in it—

boiling off as flesh from bone,
a broth to keep the bits in.

•

Is a world most complete
with creation or destruction or

just as I thought.

How much I don't know
I've forgotten

a thing holds
in its rivets.

In this ragtop body
of provisional skin

done with dreaming
I'm finished.

COLD COMFORT

If I could find just the words
to necessitate this occasion,

I'd have the golden apple
to let molder on the sill

of heaven—dull, sunless,
more or less than "cerulean"—

instead of this resonant
coffin, its silence

the tossed clod
you didn't intend

to soften the sound of the rest.

                    •

My footprint, as in footage,
is all around you, as in snow

shapes you take
to follow home.

My outline is missing—
you pulled it out

from around me
like a thread.

But nothing is lack
of anything, even that

which we don't know yet.

PROBLEM

Ephemerality of the living vs.
evanescence of remembrance:

a difference within
which I live to know

little leaves
that fuck around
the edges of an eddy.

I will not ascend
but condense into

heaven—
rafters or rooftops?

Answer: see above.

THIS SPACE

speaks volumes

into the room

we think our minds

the furthest reach

of evolution

what's visible is

the size of light.

UNI-BOMBER

Cut the wrong wire
and the timer turns back

to time (all of it
and we are coeval,

now more than ever).
Space is no better—

everything the case
is a *trompe l'oeil* stage

with real light on it.
Pantomime silence.

A poem is a robotic arm
feeling its way in the dark.

REVERSE ENGINEER

The measure of a fence
is its definition;

of my mind, its mark
in the mouth, mirroring

alluvial fans of my face.

What kind of document
is a photo of a map?

Whether I've seen a thing
whose word I'm unsure of—

say, a pergola—it's practically
certain, but I've never put

"oblivion" in a poem before.
All this time I didn't even notice.

Took almost forever,
pretty much everything

(the pickets are listing)

what I am used to
being broken.

CODICIL

My ghost has grown a lot
smaller than my outline—

ripped from ragged fabric,
holes for eyes, black

or see-through, I can't say.
In my vatic utterances of

yesterday I had 20/20
speech. I'm left a list of

indices, rattling around
in my half double helix.

·

I am what's needed
of my own erasure—

take all the empty cans
of air on top of Everest,

a hollow cairn
of barrenness

the half-moon finished
to begin with.

•

All fall the hurricanes
break up overhead,

flicker on the floor.
Far beneath, star-

nosed and crepuscular

I root for seeds
I need to grow,

bend and be
also broken.

OVER-UNDER

The whole sky changes
wherever you are

today is complete
with clouds.

Trees twist-
tie the light,

a weathervane
points its way out.

·

There must be
a perfect word

for everything or
nothing but itself.

Seen from above,
the poem is a cup;

from below, a globe
taking the world up.

•

In complete light
I have no home

to find myself here—
night is no longer

than I am in it.
My mind is made

of winter privet
you can see through

my head of breadcrumbs
to find its way home to.

WORD PROBLEMS

There are different kinds of unknowns,
including those that don't exist yet.

Potato chips, say, were created
by accident, and the unknown

of their previous non-existence has only
ever been retrospective. We have faith

in perception, assume the human brain
will grasp whatever it can access,

but exactly how much we know of what
is or might be the case is unknown.

One unifying theory holds that space
is not continuous, but made of linked

bits of it, in which case there *is* a smallest
unit of space, but the bits don't exist there,

they consist of it. Apply this to language,
where meaning is the words for it,

every word needs all the meaning
and what it is is what I'm in it for.

(If that sounds vague I know it.)
Does astronomic light white out

or decorate the dark of distance?
This, my rubbery cartoon speaker

yawping into the cosmos:
dead air

that is all
but impossible.

•

You have a mouth I keep crossing to look up. I have a
spoon in your drawer and a box of green sweetener. We
hid a six-pack in my hat and I wrote: "the choke-hold of
a river's throat." Looking back, a heron flew up it. If later
we buy a four-pack of toilet paper, two pillows and a desk
lamp, then what is the difference between the page and
what we traded with our lungs?

Answer: X=X+1

•

The absurd is a way to get around
words. Realism is only its opposite

if made to appear so. Memory
is totally realistic and unfaithful.

A poem's a Rube Goldberg doo-
hickey to elicit a flicker—I die

while I'm writing, if as yet not
of it. Do I fill with or empty of,

build or excise it?
It's a truism that truth

is found in fewest words,
which my life-shaped logo-

rrhea attests to or disproves.
Truth is to memory is to writing

what I leave you with: "being"
both noun and verb is absurd.

•

You held your hand on my mouth. I recommended dried
mangoes. All spring, a slow snow of seedlings drifted onto
the mill pond. We sat by a famous grave, a brass bar rail,
in light of your dirty kitchen: if an ancient unit coughs
out cold over a noisy traffic circle, how many stitches to
my open heart will it keep to take a beating?

Answer: Are you still with me?

•

I had another dream I couldn't read.
If you consider things on the largest

scale, how to tell the start
of a pattern from a part of it?

And what seems to be a pattern might
be a coincidence, which is funny since

they're opposites. (There are cheat codes in
the language with which we read ourselves.)

Now that cartography, say, is more
or less complete, where might the

unknowns hide in our exhaustiveness?
Quantum and cosmic are as yet

separate, but how odd that thought is
to an unknown extent effected by

their respective or collective laws.
We call all of it "physics," which

we invent or discover with our physics-
driven cognition, making ours

a recursive wisdom. Most things
have been depicted, but we'd need

every arrangement of every word
and syntactic hinge to have and hold

our capacity: a theory of everything
needs everything to contain it,

language is domestic perception,
and "God" is a name for words

for itself.

●

Smell of incense and rotten sashes. I have one coffee cup
the handle later broke from, and now you have none. Fig
Newtons. Blue curtains. Brutal mountain, prominent
forehead of flattened trees, blown matches to your kitchen
wall, where I wrote one day in surgical tape: "the view
fades / before you." This one goes out all the way, but a
horizon holds its own. How much further do I go?

Answer: Exactly nowhere at both speed and position

●

Seer and seen are not separate—
a gamma ray burst would detach

your retinas. We forget we aren't
complete, attuned to all things.

I know but hardly think of
other beings' different levels

of perception—
dogs' keen smell, whales' infra-

sonic hearing, how a hawk
can see a mole a mile away.

Each is equipped to apprehend
as needed to survive. Our sub-

species' name is *Homo sapiens sapiens*,
suggesting our self-reflexive sentience.

Language is what we feel ourselves
feeling with, and either is or makes

plain the outer rim of everything
past which we can't perceive.

"Explanatory gap" is the term
for the schism between our sensory

circuitry and how we experience it—
pain is effected by the workings

of the nervous system, but how
to explain the way it feels?

Perhaps this lack of understanding's
a lack of language. (And by "lack"

I mean both dearth and deficiency.)
(The gap is *in* the explanation and *is*

the explanation.) Is what we know
built into, also limited by, our means

of expressing it? A unit of saying is
seeing what you mean—if we could

say more might we see it? Is science
more description than explanation?

(This last may be a specious
question, but still a question.)

As our senses describe less
the world than our exigencies,

language describes itself—
this poem is my double

sapience circling itself.
I don't get the parsimony

principle: which is simpler,
God or physics? *Homo sapiens-*

*sapiens-sapiens-*ad-infinitum
will never know.

·

Over eons all the grains will be replaced but the beach
remain. Here's my imprint in it. Let's say the sand is
language and ask how much space there is together
between its units. More or less than a breadbox? Depends
how far it goes beneath. The one that came with your
kitchen, forever breadless, ringed with litter of plastic
spoons and the stainless one I gave you. He has a chicken
wrap, she a hole to heal through and another damned egg
sandwich. How far can she get on the fumes?

Answer: Every atom that belongs to me I'm going to get
back from you.

•

The smallest unit of space is made
of the same stuff as the largest,

but matter's smallest unit is
discrete. What's the biggest

unit of matter? (These questions are
not commensurate.) I have no theory

of everything, but am working on
its depiction. How to represent

it without including every thing?
I'd need a parenthetical grammar—

not progressive, but receding—
sets within sets. I want to nest

forever, but what if the nature of
everything is more an open bracket?

(My nature abhors an open bracket.)
Field theory of meaning: consciousness

is incomplete, but already all the way
here—what's missing is the size of it.

Mouth or spoon, with words we only
ever have a job to do, love

this tomb to fill up into.
Scale is a unit of measurement.

EXPLANATORY GAP

I write poems as though seeing
and knowing weren't separate—

the way they make up
the mind makes sense.

Today's sun
bent round corners,

tonight's moon
gash glares down.

What's this have to
do with reflection?

I break a mirror just to see
my shadow at the back of it.

SPECS

The world will never be
the same—

lens of last ten minutes.

Dishwater morning, gull-
colored, crying
sound of hearing itself.

With these breadcrumbs
to lead to

market, roast
beef, none—

this little hymn goes
all the way home.

•

No two words are alike,
like "snowflakes," sleet

beating down the windows.

That "alike" means "similar"
and "same" is the difference

between standing water
and sitting in it.

•

Is the point of portraiture
not to confuse
the sitter with the painter?

What I see
in the mirror

opposite me

something like
approximation.

Not one of those
heavy with fruit, more
of a stick in winter,
broken with purpose,

I err on the side
of incorrectness—

speak for the medium,
gutter the flame,

a whetstone
I sharpen
by being cut.

POSTSCRIPT

At the time of writing,
what's more important:

timeliness or verisimilitude?

I mean for you.

(A door's a door
if not open.)

Anything can be a lullaby—
what's your poison.

•

My shadow thin
as day is long

in the teeth, slung
down the street.

Stones are contained
within walls.

A dirt patch,
weak sapling

won't hold in
this wind—

the world is
a trapdoor

behind which
I reach toward.

•

Nothing is never enough,
if you count the light

length between stars.
The back of my eyes

seeing my sockets
plug into the dark—

there's only this to go on.

THE HOST

Words transubstantiate.
Fog rises

from snow, only
the word for this

is *sublimation*

(a brain contains its cranium
when you think about it).

As the darkest nights
are polluted by light

at the fringes of vision,
utter silence admits

its monstrance (sounds
worse than it is).

CENTAUR

1.

Is a wave made more
of motion or matter?

Is the answer half
of each? That seems

too exact. One rule
of science is it works

the same everywhere,
except for the words

in which it's conceived—

in other words, half
a glass is complete.

2.

A boy pulls legs
off a daddy longlegs—

shuddering black dot
stripped of its name.

Which won't regenerate.
The universe is heavier

than what we know is
in it (there's no proof

of Nietzsche having
hugged a horse, for instance).

3.

"Let's go" means either
toward or away, or—un-

contracted—"releases,"
which is just between.

Language, some believe,
is here to make us think

silence can't exist
without a word for it.

BLIVET

A poem makes much
of what's already in it

("essentially" means
"deeply" or "all but").

As swamp gas accounts
for visual phenomena

appurtenant to
the impossible:

words are fake
in fact of night,

their light the stars
won't reach to meet.

"Leave off" can mean
"stop" or "omit;"

a unicorn's an animal,
a tricorn a hat;

the beginning of a corner is
as long as you face it.

ON SPEC

What's more opaque:
mirror or milk glass?

Depends what happens
at the end (in your face).

My eyes milk up
with cataracts.

(What you think
you're looking at?)

All I know is that
much is apparent—

a surface turns
as needed to seem.

DEPT. OF THE INTERIOR

Do you see through
or only into sky?

Nature abhors
a preposition.

Sky has no eyes
to see, isn't even

blue but seems it.

Space is room
it keeps for you.

RHUMB LINE

Language is made
to make you think

it's been here forever—

the object of which
is not to be

understood?

•

In a berth belowdecks,
waves' hollow slap

against hull, the creak
of salted rope. A bell

buoy's *bong*
of distance—

all night long
another begins.

•

How many points
make up the globe?

Each second is
an antipode.

As death and life
are not opposites,

but twins—
their difference isn't

in them, but the words
to think it/with.

AS EVER

How much time do I hold
at any moment?

Just think of it—

why am I still not infinite?

All I know but won't tell
from the back of the tapestry

(can't burn
a burning thing).

The forest on fire
I don't see behind this tree.

•

I have a vestigial
origin in my eye,

forever closing
nesting doors.

A gold-leaf
box of gold,

the head a hinge
it opens with.

•

Is what I want more
a way out or way in?

Words close like key-
holes with keys in them.

You there, in the tower—

let down your shadows
to climb out of.

Each time I find my way inside
I'm shown the missing door.

AUTOMAT

... perhaps you show the way things look the less you show how they are or how we think they are.

—Richard Estes

•

Please pardon our appearance
while we improve our store
of skyline in X-Acto-ed blue
born of roofs, clouds bound
where they are going, there
but for the eye. Time here
appears to be its opposite
(is plate glass full or empty
of itself)? It takes a moment
to think about it. A window is
filled with the shape of its limit—
you have to see through this—
we're split from the world
by being born to it.

•

When they rolled the stone away
the tomb was taken up with itself.
A dome rises sideways
from vertical horizon, white
winter light, scrim of thin clouds
in front of another. In the unseen
ground beneath, window boxes
of glass flowers housing bees,
neat stacks of window envelopes.
As "appear" can mean "materialize"
or "dissimulate," leaning, at odds
with the horizontal lines,
the maker looks far away
from our eyes.

●

Please pardon our appearance
here, piecing rivets,
stitched apart into
Perseus holding himself
to the mirror. Holy mess
of a tangram, where
same figures contain
each other—and words,
do they contain us as
well, we'll just have to see.
Poems are holey. A façade
bends away from the face.
I can see myself saying
that what breaks from you
remains.

•

When they rolled the stone
away, nothing left
to see through. See-
through wings of this
butterflied day, splayed
on its scope: the world's
camouflage for windows.
(Should I want to close
or fill the distance?)
Lateness lasts long
before it begins—
backwards virgin,
today is an indent
to take your time in.

Please pardon our appearance
in a parallel light, lined up
with fluorescent tubes. Waiting-
room-blue upstages the ocean.
While I've been known
to throw a sea in for scale,
this one has nothing on
the length of intersecting it.
In the divining of eyes,
sextant stars, the nave of my age
imperceptible and streaming
through the clerestory,
all that I see
is the window behind me.

•

When they roll the stone away,
I am less who I am than I used to be.
Falling leaves make branches
of boughs, fold into the lens
to become the picture.
I'd love nothing more
in the mirror (double
doors with wet bits
banked against them).
Limb from limb, we grow
away, as blind spiders
back into a cave—
this view has a room
how far in front of you.

•

Please pardon our missing
appearance from the picture—
a gunwale cuts through scum
wake to torn construction-
paper island. Up through
hole, around the tree, back
into it, the rope. Last time
I tied a bowline (it's easy
to undo after bearing a load)
on my neck, nearly choked
the engine. Suggested
sign reads NO WAKE,
meaning go slow—so
sorry this never happens.

●

When they roll the stone
from the cave, remains
invisible on either side.
Doubled over chrome
stools, asswards words
name how you think
they're distinct from the glass,
but nothing's there
to cast them—automat red,
boxy blue, reflections look
like what they're made of.
File by the open tomb
with windows there
to see this through.

•

Please pardon our appearance
stacked against us—glass
falls clear from nowhere.
Before you can be seen
fill out these forms, all
small sucking sounds
of dancers' feet un-
sticking to the floor
in aural tangrams of exteriority.
Check the box for negative
space or by-product, depiction
of an image or models who
paint back at you.
A frame sets off itself.

•

When they rolled the stone away
what ragged form tore out.
Slow cloud rises from site
of detonation: edifice,
collapse and aftermath
co-create a plume of ash,
the nib to write it with.
Take my word for what
ails you in the mouth—spit
images as glass, a dicta-
phonic, *You should be in pictures.*
What's a photorealistic poem?
A: "Abstract." There's a crack
in the world where the eye goes.

ACKNOWLEDGMENTS

Poems from this manuscript have appeared in *The Awl, Barrelhouse, Bennington Review, Boston Review, The Brooklyn Rail, Café Review, Columbia Poetry Review, The Elephants, New American Writing, Oversound, Thin Air, Tupelo Quarterly and The Volta*. Many thanks to the editors of these publications.

The astronomic light on p. 34 is borrowed from George Oppen.

This book would not exist without the friendship and meticulous attention of Darcie Dennigan and Kate Schapira. For various forms of support and inspiration I am also grateful to Mary-Kim Arnold, Christina Davis, Fanny Howe, Lynn Melnick, Peter Middleton, Ryan Murphy, Todd Shalom, Han VanderHart, and Karen Weiser.

Thank you most of all to my family—Rusty, Willie and Maggie—to whom I dedicate this book.

ABOUT THE AUTHOR

Kate Colby's eight previous books of poetry and prose include *I Mean* and *Dream of the Trenches*. She has received awards and fellowships from the Poetry Society of America, Rhode Island State Council for the Arts, the Dodd Research Center at University of Connecticut, and Harvard's Woodberry Poetry Room. She lives in Providence.

Lightning Source UK Ltd.
Milton Keynes UK
UKHW012121070223
416656UK00005B/15